CW01509905

The
Beloved

[-adj, much loved.
  n, much loved person.]

Design of this book by Nancy Goudie and Chris Mathison. Series design by Helen Martin.

Cover and interior illustrations by Charlotte Cooke.

Published by The NGM Trust, Caedmon Complex, Bristol Road, Thornbury, BS35 3JA. www.ngm.org.uk

Printed by TJ Books, Padstow, Cornwall.

Preface

This book contains a collection of real stories, poems, wise words, meditations, love songs and huge encouragement to know that you are God's beloved child.

Throughout this book I pray that you will hear God's whisper in your ear that he is so in love with you. I am praying that you will see through the content of this book that you are an amazing creation and a person of great value. Not many of us see ourselves in this way, yet you are someone who has been called and chosen and you are loved unconditionally. You are beautiful and God is well pleased with you.

Any time you feel down, unloved or critical of yourself; any time someone speaks an unkind word to you or life hits you hard, then pick up this book and flick through its pages. Each page is filled with the truth of who you are. Each page is designed to bring you words of encouragement and hope. Pick any page and read it whilst allowing what you read to restore your joy and build up your soul. Also in this expanded edition, you will find promises to you from God. He is the one who always fulfils his promises. He won't let you down, so read his words, believe them and watch them come into being. Take this book with you wherever you go. Leave a copy beside your bed and remind yourself before you go to sleep just how special and precious you are!

A Note from Nancy

Did you know that there are over 8000 promises in the Bible and each one will come into being? Some promises are for specific people but others are more general and we can claim each one of those promises for ourselves. I don't know about you, but I take promises very seriously. When someone doesn't follow through on one of their promises it can be very hard to take. Children, in particular never forget what someone has promised them. They may forget to tidy their room, or make their bed, or put away their toys, but when a someone says they will do something, they will remember it until it is fulfilled. Many times, you will hear children saying to their parents, But Mum, Dad you promised!!! Be careful what you say in reply because if you say, *"Well….let's wait and see!"* In their mind that means YES. Even if you say, I'm not sure that can happen or I will look and see! That too means YES. Promises are very important and God thinks so too. He never breaks a promise – he fulfils each one. You can count on each of his promises for he is faithful – always!

This book when it was originally released in 2009 it was designed to show you that you are God's Beloved. **He absolutely adores you.** He loves you so much and that is true whether you reject him or accept him. He never stops loving you. You are his precious and incredible child. He adores you!

This extended book is to assure you too of the promises of God over your life and to remind you that God not only loves you but he has promised you many thousands of promises. He won't fail you; he will fulfil every one of his promises to you! Our God is faithful.

One of his promises to you is that he will never leave you nor will he forsake you (Deut 31:8). No matter where you go, he will be with you. You can count on that even when you don't feel him around you, or perhaps you feel all alone – the truth is he is with you! He has promised and he will not fail you.

Some of his promises in the Bible are conditional like Philippians 4:6-7. Do not be anxious about anything, but in everything by prayer and petition with thanksgiving present your requests to God and the peace of God which transcends all understanding will guard your hearts and minds in Christ Jesus. What a promise when we pray and thank God for situations that are worrisome. This is how it is written in The Living Bible… Do not worry about anything; instead, pray about everything. Tell God what you need, and don't forget to thank him for all he has done. Then you will experience God's peace, which exceeds anything we can understand. His peace will guard your hearts and minds as you live in Christ Jesus. What a wonderful promise to each of us – but it is conditional on us not worrying, but praying with a thankful heart for all he has done and will do for you. If you do that, then you will receive his peace and his joy. This is one of God's promises to you.

As you read this book, my prayer is that you will see how loved you are and how many promises have been given to you. I hope the promises of God encourage you to trust him for today, tomorrow and forever.

Also, one of the gifts that God has given me is to be able to listen to the Lord and write down what I believe the Lord is saying to a particular person. I do this every year at my Spiritual Health Weekend. During the year as people book into my Spiritual Health Weekend, their name is placed on a list and as a team we pray for these people every week. However, as well as this, I take this list and go through it every day with the Lord asking the Lord for a promise and a word from him to every individual person. When they come to the Spiritual Health Weekend, that word is put on a card and is read over them. Always when the individual receives this word, they are blown away by the special word for them on the card. The accuracy of the word sometimes astounds people. One lady asked her friend why she told me (Nancy) about her. Her friend said she had not told me anything about this lady. The lady said, *"Then read this"* – and gave her the card to read and said, *"How did Nancy know this if you didn't tell her?"* Her reply was, *"Nancy doesn't know about you, but God does."* My words from God to the ladies who attend my weekend are always encouraging. They talk about how much God loves them, but also it may contain some things that only the person receiving the word and the Lord would know.

I remember getting a word from God for someone and the word said, 'God says, you are not small, he sees you as ten foot tall'. Several times I repeated that phrase throughout the word and stated that God saw her as significant. I was feeling that the person was always feeling inadequate because of the way she saw herself. When the team member took the word to this person, she could not believe what she saw. The person was very small – I think, if I remember correctly, that she was under 5 foot.

I also remember when a friend of mine came and told me that she always valued the words that God gave me for her, however this time she did not like the word. The word talked about 'even if the worst happens, that he would be there for her'. He wanted to assure my friend that He would always be with her through the easy and the worst times of life. However, she didn't want the worst to happen. I told her perhaps the word was not for now, but was for a time in the future. Or maybe I didn't hear God clearly enough and perhaps I was wrong. She took the word and put it in her Bible and never looked at it again. A few years later, she went through a really tough time – the worst time ever! She sat down with her Bible and cried out to God to speak to her. At that point, the card I had given her fell out of her Bible. She picked it up and what she read brought comfort and help in the middle of the trauma she was going through. The Lord encouraged her hugely – He had not forgotten her; he was with her even when the worst happened.

Today as I am continuing to write this book, I saw a comment on Facebook that a lady I don't know wrote to me. She had attended my Spiritual Health Weekend about 20 years ago. She said, *"I recall Nancy's word she had for me at least 20 years ago telling me that I would live to see the grey hairs on my head! Even after a terminal cancer diagnosis! Thank you for those words, Nancy! God is good."* I wrote back telling her I just write what I hear God say and

I trust that I am hearing clearly from God. Isn't it wonderful that God gave me that word just when she was needing to hear it. I didn't know she was going to get a terminal cancer diagnosis which would be so bad for her that she could hardly walk without being sick. Yet here she is 20 years later! Lord I am so in awe of you!

This gift of being able to hear God's prophetic voice for others is so special. What a privilege to be able to do that. It takes me all year to hear a word from God for every woman who books into my Spiritual Health Weekend (between 450 – 600 individual people), but it is so worthwhile. So, I thought I would reach out to the Lord for some prophetic words for people reading this book. So, amongst the many wonderful promises within this book there are also some prophetic words for you from the Lord. I really hope they encourage and bless you hugely, especially at the right time. As you hear God's promises for you my prayer is that you will trust God more fully than ever before.

"My precious people, listen to my voice. I have called you by name – you are mine! You are precious and honoured in my sight and I adore you (Isaiah 43:1). I have loved you from before the world was created. I have called and chosen you to see great things happen in my name (Ephesians 1:4). Look for those who have eyes but are blind. Show them the way to go. Do not be afraid to use your voice to call them even when they are deaf for my words will penetrate their heart and their mind. Know the depths of my love for this world and remember that you are my witnesses (Isaiah 43:8-10). I am the Saviour of the world, apart from me, there is no

other Saviour (Isaiah 43:11). Call to me and I will answer you. Do not hold back, instead seek me and you will find me (Jeremiah 29:13). I am your Jehovah Jireh, your provider. I provide you with everything you need for life and for godliness (2 Peter 1:3). Do not be afraid, but instead trust in me for all things. Call to me and I will show you the way to go, and when that happens take people with you and show them the way to go too. My precious people, know my voice and keep following me for I have much for you. I am your provider, your great God who will guard you and keep you. I am your God; your wonderful promise keeper. Trust in me and see all I will do for you."

I believe God wants each reader to know this truth:

He loves you; he adores you; he will never leave you and his promises are for you today and every day.

Trust him in the midst of the storm for he is your God and he never fails. Trust him always for he is there for you. He never fails you.

Woohoo!

THE BELOVED

"Let the beloved of the Lord rest secure in him
for he shields him all day long,
and the one the Lord loves rests
between his shoulders."

Deuteronomy 33:12

You are God's beloved!
Today, remember he shields you all day long
therefore take time to rest your weary head
on his chest.

God's promises
and <u>special words for you</u>:

> *Even to your old age and grey hairs – I am he, I am he*
> *who will sustain you and I will rescue you.*
>
> (Isaiah 46:4)

God's promises for you are not just for when you are young,
but also when you are old. He never discards you for you
are his Beloved. He loves you, in fact, he adores you! His
blessing remains on you always. As you go through life,
he is with you. As you travel from young to old, he never
leaves you. His presence remains with you. He loves you
when you are young and he loves you when you are old.
He sustains you when you are young and continues to do
so when you are old. Can you fail with Jesus on your side?
Never – for he will turn any bad situation into good for you
as you keep on loving and praising him.

What a Saviour!
What a God!

He is faithful and loving to us all no matter how old we are!

God's promises
and special words for you:

"My peace I give to you – not as the world gives, but the peace I have - I give it to you. In fact, I already have given to you; remember that when you long to taste my peace you already have it. Sink down deep into my peace and know the peace that passes all understanding. The same peace that I knew when faced with betrayal, jealousy, hurt and darkness is there for you now. Thank me for my gift of peace to you. It's a gift that will never fail you. Trust me as you sink deep into the love and grace that brings you immense peace."

Breath of Life

This is a great blessing to read over your life regularly. This is how God sees you – his amazingly beautiful child!

Do you not know how perfectly you have been made? Do you not know how wonderfully special you are? You are crafted to perfection even in the smallest detail. You are beautiful from head to toe, beautiful beyond compare; absolutely flawless. Your beauty shines like the sun in the sky!

Receive the love and grace being poured out upon you. Receive the oil of joy as I pour it upon your soul. Let the perfume of my love soak into your mind. Receive the fragrance of my smile let it penetrate deep within. Take what is rightfully yours. Let my words bring you deep healing as I pour these oils and perfumes upon you.

I want you to know there is much ahead for you. There are treasures beyond belief. There's an inheritance of good things stored up for you. Keep looking; keep searching; keep asking and listening and good things will come to you. Reach for the best and believe for the best; for they will be yours.

There are many treasures stored up for you. Open your heart and receive them now. Stand underneath the fountain of blessings and be drenched in love.'

Extract from 'The Prayer of Blessing' © Nancy Goudie 2008. Smile (meditation CD). Published by MCS Music Ltd/Curious? Music UK/ngm

How Does God See Us?

You're beautiful from head to toe, my dear love,
beautiful beyond compare, absolutely flawless!

Song of Songs 4:7 (The Message)

You have stolen my heart, my sister, my bride;
you have stolen my heart with one glance of your eyes.

Song of Songs 4:9

My lover spoke and said to me,
"Arise, my darling, my beautiful one
and come with me."

Song of Songs 2:10

How beautiful you are, my darling!
Oh how beautiful!

Song of Songs 4:1

There is no-one like her on the earth, never has been,
never will be. She is a woman beyond compare. My
dove is perfection, pure and innocent as the day she was
born and cradled in joy by her mother.

Song of Songs 6:9 (The Message)

Let's see ourselves the way God sees us!

His Song of Joy For You

Did you know that God rejoices over you?
Did you know that his heart constantly sings
songs of love over you?
Did you know that his delight is in you?
Never forget how special you are to God!

The Lord your God is with you,
he is mighty to save.
He will take great delight in you,
he will quiet you with his love,
he will rejoice over you with singing.

Zephaniah 3:17

Special

To feel special is to feel loved.
To feel loved is to know you are special.
To know you are special is to know God as your Father, your
Abba, your Daddy and his great love for you.

You have been born into God's family – you are his special
child. He has lavished his love upon you!

*How great is the love the Father has lavished on us, that we
should be called children of God!*
And that is what we are!

1 John 3:1

As the Father has loved me, so have I loved you.
Now remain in my love

John 15:9

God's promises
and special words for you:

> *What I have said that will I bring about; what I have*
> *planned that will I do.*
>
> (Isaiah 46:11b)

His word is faithful and true. You can trust him always. If God, the living God has said it, then it will happen. Trust him through the questions and trust him through the pain. What he has planned will happen. There is no doubt about it. Even when it is too late, it's not too late for him. In John 11, it tells us that Jesus didn't turn up when his best friend (Lazurus) was ill. He didn't even attend the funeral. Mary and Martha couldn't understand it. Why didn't he come? They knew Lazurus was one of his closest friends and that he loved him. So why didn't he come? When he eventually arrived Martha and Mary thought he was too late. They had loads of questions as to why he didn't turn up, but then they discovered that Jesus wasn't too late and in fact he was right on time to see a miracle happen and to do the will of the Father. If God has said it will happen, then it will happen. Trust him through the pain and the darkness to see the miracle God has planned.

What an amazing miracle!

Do Not Worry!

We so often spend our days and nights worrying about various issues, some of which happen and others that only might happen. This type of stress is not good for our health; physical, emotional or mental health. Listen to the advice Jesus gives us!

"Therefore I tell you, do not worry about your life, what you will eat or drink; or about your body, what you will wear. Is not life more important than food, and the body more important than clothes?

Look at the birds of the air; they do not sow or reap or store away in barns, and yet your heavenly Father feeds them. Are you not much more valuable than they? Who of you by worrying can add a single hour to his life?"

Matthew 6:25 – 27

Let's make up our minds not to worry! Each time a worry comes into your mind, see yourself give it to Jesus. Then train your mind to turn away from your worrying thoughts, by deliberately thinking of something positive and good.

God's promises
and <u>special words for you:</u>

> *For God so loved the world that he gave his one and only son, that whoever believes in him shall not perish but have eternal life. For God did not send his son to condemn the world, but to save the world through him.*
>
> John 3:16-17

These two verses are incredible. Do you feel condemned in this life? Then this did not come from God. Conviction is different to condemnation. Our own conscious can convict us which should lead us to repentance and forgiveness, but condemnation which only comes from the enemy only shames and damages the person. Jesus did not come into the world to condemn the world, but to show the love and forgiveness of the Father and to show that you and me can have eternal life no matter what we have done, if we believe in Jesus Christ – the Saviour of the world and ask him into our lives. Through Jesus life, death and resurrection we can have life and have it in all its fulness (John 10:10). For this reason, the son, Jesus, came into the world. This is the greatest promise. Take a hold of this promise today and receive what God has promised which is eternal life because of Jesus.

My glorious and wonderful son/daughter, today know for certain that if you believe in my son, Jesus Christ, and believe that he lived, died and rose again and that he did this to make a way for you to come into a relationship with me, then you are indeed my child; you are in my family and you are mine always. When that time happened and you opened up your heart to me, then your future and your forever home was certain. Trust me and trust in my word. Jesus was not sent to condemn you, but to give you an opportunity to receive the gift of eternal life.

I love you, my child.
I am always with you and I
rejoice over you.

(Zephaniah 3:17)

God's promises
and special words for you:

> *Do not let your heart be troubled. Trust in God; trust also in me (Jesus). In my Father's house are many rooms, if it were not so, I would have told you. I go to prepare a place for you, and I will come back and take you to be with me that you also may be where I am going.*
>
> (John 14:1-4)

My beautiful and precious child, I want you to know that I do not leave you as an orphan (John 14:18). Do not let your heart be troubled. I speak my peace to you, my special one. It's not just any peace; it's my peace – the peace that passes all understanding. Trust in me and know that I am here right now. I am preparing for you a special place and I will come back and take you to be with me. You are important to me. I have always covered you with my love. Before you were born, I loved you and called you to be mine. Listen to my voice and put your trust in me. Never forget how much I love and adore you. **You are important!**

peace

Over flowing Joy

Though many trials and heartaches
Try and stop me sing
I can't deny the truth and love
His warm affection brings
He's called me his beloved one
In whom he is well pleased
His grace, forgiveness poured on me
His blessings never cease

Overflowing joy in my heart
Overflowing joy in my soul
Amazing love so wonderful
Has got a hold on me
Overflowing hope in my heart
Overflowing hope in my soul
I know you hold the future
And I know you hold my hand
Overflowing joy

Holy Spirit fall on me
Enlarge my heart of love
Let my passion reach the skies
With angels high above
I choose to trust you everyday
And stay with you always
Please clothe me with your presence
I will love you all my days

Lyrics by Ray Goudie. Song recorded on 'Your Kingdom Come'.
Published by ngm admin/Daybreak music/Fierce! Publishing 2008

God's promises
and <u>special words for you:</u>

Has God Forgotten Me?

God's answer is always –
"I could never forget you!"

"CAN A MOTHER FORGET THE BABY AT HER
BREAST AND HAVE NO COMPASSION ON THE
CHILD SHE HAS BORNE? THOUGH SHE MAY
FORGET, I WILL NOT FORGET YOU. SEE, I HAVE
ENGRAVED YOU ON THE PALMS OF MY HANDS;
YOU ARE FOREVER BEFORE ME."

Isaiah 49:15-16

23

God's promises
and special words for you:

> *Weeping may last for a night, but joy comes in the morning.*
>
> (Psalm 30:5)

What a promise......I know this to be true – when my
husband died in 2016, I lost a most precious man – my soul
mate, my best friend, my husband, my valentine, my lover
and my most intimate partner.......I was devastated – I was
broken – I mourned deeply, yet that night when I told God
I trusted him for the future without Ray, when I didn't have
the answer to all my questions God gave me two beautiful
gifts. I told him I had a hundred and one different questions and no answers for any of them. I then went on to say,
*"However, I know I am not called to understand everything,
but I am called to trust you and trust you is what I am going to
do."* I spoke those words out loud to the Lord in my bedroom beside the same bed that my husband's body had just
been taken away from by the undertakers. God gave me his
peace – not just any peace or an earthly peace, but his peace
- the peace that passes all understanding. The other gift he
gave me is what I called a bubble of joy. I felt it bubbling up
within me. I didn't understand! How could I have this joy
whilst I was in mourning – yet I had it. Of course, the Bible
tells us that he promises to turn our mourning into joy (Jeremiah 31:13). God honoured his promises when I trusted in
Him. If he has been able to give these gifts to me, then he

can give them to you. It didn't stop me mourning, but those precious gifts helped me whilst I was mourning. Trust him and receive his gifts of peace and joy.

"My precious and beautiful child, I want you to know that I see your tears and know your fears, but as you trust in me, I will honour my promise of joy. Your weeping may last for a while, but I promise to give you my peace (John 14:27) and my joy (John 15:11). These gifts have already been given to you and when you trust in me you will know and feel that peace and joy. My peace and my joy have been released to you, enjoy living in the beauty of the life I have promised you (John 10:10)."

The Riches of His Grace

When storms come across your bow
always remember that God is with you.
Remember that he has promised to give you the treasures
of darkness; riches stored in secret places so that you may
know God and that your trust in him will develop and
grow to greater lengths than ever before.

(Isaiah 45:3)

For great is your love, higher than the heavens;
Your faithfulness reaches to the skies.

Psalm 108:4

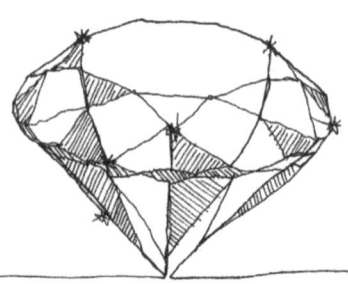

A Hug from God

Do you not know how much I love you?

Do you not know how much I care?

I have wrapped my strong arms around you and have hugged you close to my heart. (Isaiah 40:11)

I deeply care for you!

I love you with an everlasting love!

Yet, my child, my beloved child, you have not yet experienced the full expression of my love.

Open your heart and open your mouth and I will fill you to overflowing.

Trust in me for I have much for you.

God's promises
and special words for you:

I lift up my eyes to the hills –
where does my help come from?
My help comes from the Lord,
the Maker of heaven and earth.

He will not let your foot slip –
he who watches over you will not slumber;
indeed, he who watches over Israel
will neither slumber nor sleep.

The Lord watches over you –
the Lord is your shade at your right hand;
the sun will not harm you by day
nor the moon by night.

The Lord will keep you from all harm –
he will watch over your life;
the Lord will watch over your coming and
going
both now and for evermore.

Psalm 121

Our God is amazing!

20 Beautiful Things
that are true about you...

1 You are unique, special, one of a kind; there is no-one in the world who is exactly like you.

2 You are loved completely and utterly. No-one is more loved than you!

3 You are beautiful beyond compare!

4 You are gifted. God has liberally given you gifts.

5 You shine like the stars in the sky; you sparkle like a pure cut diamond.

6 When you smile you radiate God's glory.

7 The amazing fragrance of your life spreads to everyone around.

8 You have the ability within you to love the unloved.

9 You have a wonderful mind that can retain thoughts, dreams and memories; better than any computer!

10 You have the ability within you to forgive, love and cherish those who have hurt you.

11 Your laughter can change the world around you.

12 You have a friend who is closer than a brother or sister.

13 You have an inner strength within you; dig deep and you will find it.

14 Joy is placed within you; but even if you lose your joy you can always find it again.

15 You can sing and make melodies in your heart.

16 You can pray and communicate spiritually; only humans can do this!

17 Just by being in the world means you make a special contribution to life.

18 There is always space in your heart for others; even if you don't realise it.

19 You have the ability to see beyond the natural.

20 You have the favour of God upon you.

God's promises
and <u>special words for you:</u>

I am the way, the truth and the life

John 14: 6

The Son of God says that he will lead you for he is the way. He is the truth – he will always speak truth to you. Jesus tells us in John 8:44 that the enemy's native language is lies, but God always speaks truth to you. Quieten your heart and mind and listen to the man of truth. He brings you life – for he is life. He promised you abundant life through his promise in John 10:10 – I have come to bring life, life in its fullest sense.

"My precious and amazing one, trust in me now and forevermore. I am the way, the truth and the life no one comes to the Father, but through me (John14:6). Come to me and I will show you greater things than you have ever seen. I tell you the truth, anyone who has faith in me will do what I have been doing. In fact, you will do even greater things because I am going to the Father. I will do whatever you ask

*in my name. You may ask me for anything
in my name and I will do it! If you love
me, then you will obey what I command.
(John 14:13-15). Come to me and I will give
you eternal life and the Father will give
you another Counsellor to be with you
forever – the Spirit of truth. The world
cannot accept him because it neither sees
him or knows him, but you will know him,
for he will live within you. I will never
leave you as orphans (John 14:15-18). My
precious one I am with you always. I will
show you the way, the truth and the life.
Trust in me."*

My Special One

Such joy fills my heart when I look at you!
I have no regrets or disappointments in you.
You think you are weak, but I know you are strong.
Your strength comes from my joy;
fill your heart with my joy.
Rejoice in who you are;
one filled with beauty and grace.
You are my special one and I want you to know
you are loved and adored
And you will be always!

Stay 'at Home' with God

He who dwells in the shelter of the Most High
will rest in the shadow of the Almighty.
I will say of the Lord, "He is my refuge and my fortress
my God, in whom I trust."

Psalm 91:1-2

Be a permanent house guest of the throne room of God. In his presence you will always find joy and rest. Trust him in all your ways for he will never let you down or let you go.

He is our Protection

For the Lord God is a sun and a shield;
The Lord bestows favour and honour
No good thing does he withhold
From those whose walk is blameless

Psalm 84:11

Listen to me...
you whom I have upheld since you were conceived,
and have carried since your birth.
Even to your old age and grey hairs I am he,
I am he who will sustain you.
I have made you and I will carry you;
I will sustain you and I will rescue you.

Isaiah 46:3-4

Listen my child, I will never let you go. Do not fear evil
for I am with you. I am at your right hand and I will never
forsake you. I will love you and protect you forever. My
embrace is always on you. Never fear for I am here always!

Priceless

No matter what you go through in life, always remember I am with you. I will never leave you for you are priceless in my sight.

When you pass through the waters,
I will be with you;
And when you pass through the rivers,
they will not sweep over you,
When you walk through the fire,
you will not be burned;
the flames will not set you ablaze.
For I am the Lord, your God.

Isaiah 43:2-3a

My son had been naughty! I cannot remember what he had done, but I do remember the look on his face when he had been found out. He could not look me in the eye and the horror of disobeying was displayed all over his face. I hugged and told him, "Even though you have been naughty I still deeply love you!" I will never forget the shocked look that came into his eyes. He could not believe that his Mum and his Dad could still love him. I went on to say "No matter what you do, Dad and I will always love you. We are saddened that you did something wrong, but our love for you remains the same."

Our love for our children is just a small reflection of how God loves us. Isn't it wonderful to know that God loves us unconditionally? Even when we do things wrong, he still deeply loves us!

What Love!

There is nothing we can do to make God love us less.
There is nothing we can do to make Him love us more.
He loves us completely, unconditionally and fully.
His love is magnificent and totally breath-taking.
How wonderful is that!

God's Delight is in You

I want you to know that you delight my heart. You make me sing with joy (Zephaniah 3:17). You are like a beautiful diamond; shining for all to see. All who look and observe your beauty are stunned at how lovingly you have been made. You were crafted and woven together by my hands. From before the world began I loved you and knew you (Ephesians 1:4). Sing, oh my beloved. Lift up your voice and rejoice, for you are wonderful and you are mine (Isaiah 43:1).

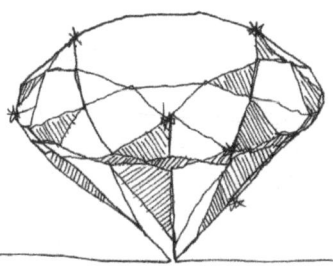

God's promises
and special words for you:

> *God will be your bodyguard and protect you when trouble is near*
>
> (Psalm 34:20 -TPT)

I love this verse about God being our bodyguard. We see in our world that many celebrities and royal family members have bodyguards, but do you recognise that you and me have the best bodyguard ever? God is our bodyguard and he protects us especially when trouble is near. I love that. This promise gives me confidence in my life, especially now that my husband of 43 years is no longer here in this world. Since 2016 I have had to live life without my best friend, my husband. He wasn't much of a bodyguard to be honest – he was only 5 foot 8 inches and didn't have many muscles, but I know he would have gone with me anywhere. Today my best friend, my constant companion is also my bodyguard. He walks with me wherever I go in life. I have to constantly remind myself of this fact when I have to walk into a crowded room, a restaurant or indeed anywhere on my own. It takes courage to do that, and I find it hard to do, but when I remember that I am not alone I can walk in with confidence knowing that my bodyguard is beside me.

Remind yourself that your bodyguard is with you. He is at your right-hand side (Psalm 16:8). He is at your left-hand side in fact he completely surrounds you (Psalm 125:2). He goes before you and is behind you (Psalm 139:2). If you are a Christian and have accepted Jesus into your life, then he lives inside you (2 Cor 13:5 and also Galatians 2:20) and you live inside of him (Acts 17:28 and John 15:4). What a wonderful promise for us to claim, but to get the full protection of God in Heaven, we need to make sure we are trusting in him by asking him to come into our life and following his ways.

You are a Treasure

"You are my beloved treasured possession.
I will never discard you!
You fill my heart with overflowing joy!"

The Lord God has chosen you out of all the peoples on the face of the earth to be... his treasured possession.

Deuteronomy 7:6

I looked and I saw a vessel filled with all kinds of treasures – gold, silver, jewels and diamonds! It was full to overflowing. I saw the Lord gently take you, his beloved, by the hand and lead you to this treasure. As he did he spoke and said "My child, all you see is yours! Don't just look, but come and enjoy all I have for you."

Be overwhelmed with God's love, grace and provision for you his amazing child!

Clothes of Love

I have placed a ring on your finger and lovingly called you my own.

(Luke 15:22-23)

I have dressed you with garments of salvation and robes of righteousness.

(Isaiah 61:10)

There is no good thing I would not do for you!

(Psalm 84:11)

Spend a few minutes to imagine you clothing yourself with his clothes of love.

Love is...

patient walking away from envy

being together
not easily angered kind

not self seeking

not proud not delighted in evil

special not boastful

not keeping a record of wrongs

forgiving intimate

not rude

faithful always hopeful

always thinking the best

never failing truthful

tender hearted trusting

caring for the poor

standing up against injustice

always encouraging

never giving up

always there ...GOD

Our Passionate Lover - Jesus

There is no love like the love of Jesus.
He goes the extra mile;
he climbs the highest mountain;
he overcomes all obstacles
in order that you his beloved
might know his love.

Diamond

Knowing that we are loved and accepted is something that is essential to all of us. There is a need deep within us to know that we are loved and valued. We can at times be hard on ourselves, feeling that we do not quite hit the mark; that we are not quite accepted by ourselves never mind others.

If you feel the need to know you are loved; if you have feelings of loneliness or pain at being alone, then come with me as we explore the truth about who we are.

Close your eyes and begin to see a man walking in a field. As he looks down to the ground, he sees something sparkling from the earth. As he bends down to examine it closely he realises he has found a beautifully crafted diamond. As he gently wipes the dirt away and as the stone shines, he realises this is a diamond of immense value. He carefully puts the diamond back into the ground and then goes and sells everything he has in order to buy the whole field. It doesn't matter to him how much it costs for he knows the field contains the beautiful diamond. Once the field is bought, the diamond is then his. How valuable was that diamond! It cost him everything, yet his joy was complete.

As you watch the picture, hear the man of truth speak to your heart. "You are that beautiful exquisite diamond. You shine like the sun in the sky sending your beautiful fragrance far and wide. You are not ugly, unloved or rejected. You are not forgotten or abandoned, for I will never leave you nor forsake you. You are beautiful, absolutely flawless.

While you were in your mother's womb, I fashioned you and chose you. You have been loved from before you were born. I know sometimes you feel forgotten and unloved. Thoughts come to you – does anyone care? I care and always will do. Can a mother forget the baby at her breast? Though she may forget, I will not forget you. You are beautiful beyond compare. I have bought you with a huge price. When I looked and saw how much you were worth, I chose you and chose to set you free to enjoy life in all its fullness. Enjoy living in the freedom I have given you. You are special!"

So any time you feel tired, down, unloved and not cared for, remember the truth – remember you are special, you are valuable, you have been bought with a price and you are and you always will be surrounded by love.

Extract from 'Smile' (meditation CD) © Nancy Goudie 2008. Published by MCS Music Ltd/Curious? Music UK/ngm

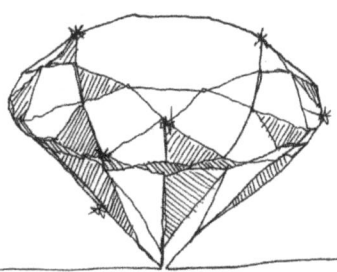

God's promises
and special words for you:

No one can pluck you from my hand

John 10:27-28

You are safe in the hands of God. Nothing and no one can steal you away from safety in God's hands. Isn't this wonderful? The enemy will tell you that you are not going to see God move in your life and in your situation. He will try and remove you from God's wonderful care – but he cannot do that. Only you can remove yourself from the Lord's care. Don't walk away from the Lord – instead stay where you are safe and covered in love. Stay where you are, safe in the hand of the Lord God. *"My beautiful one, do not fear, instead settle down and stay safe in my hands. I have promised to save you and save you I will. Trust in me, rest in my love. Know the depth of my love for you. You are safe with me. I adore you. I cover you with my love. Sink into the safety of my waters and know the love and grace in which I cover you. My beautiful one, you are safe with me."*

Arms of Grace

O Lord, what can I say?
I'm here again to tell my story
I feel so far away
How I long to hear your words of love calling me

You know you so amaze me
The way you keep on always loving
The way you stay so close
And I just can't stop my broken heart from chasing you

Let me run into your arms of grace
To say "I'm sorry
For the things I have done."
And I fall into your warm embrace
Let me say, let me say "I'm sorry,
And I love you forevermore."

You make me feel so safe
You take me to another place
I feel your love again
How I long to stay so close to you forever

I know you're always there
And in my darkest times you're by my side
I feel a deep desire
And I know that I can make it through with you

©1999 Ian Townend/Ray Goudie

You are not a 'Loser'!

With God on our side, how can we lose? If God didn't hesitate to put everything on the line for us, embracing our condition and exposing himself to the worst by sending his own Son, is there anything else he wouldn't gladly and freely do for us?

Romans 8:31-32 (The Message)

If God is for us – who can be against us?

Romans 8:31

I'm Wild About You!

A number of years ago I heard a story about a nun who attended a seminar of a well known speaker. The speaker was leading people in spiritual exercises. He gave them a Christian meditation to do and then asked for some feedback. The nun asked if she could share what she had experienced. She said, "The moment you told us to close our eyes, I saw a picture of myself sitting on a chair at the edge of a dance floor. A man came up to me and asked me to dance. I raised my head to say 'No thanks', but when I looked into his eyes I found myself saying yes and walking with him to the dance floor.

When we started to dance it was as if we were made for each other. We turned, twirled and danced so well together that the others on the dance floor all stopped dancing and watched us. I thought to myself, *"Who is this man? Who is this one who has captured my heart? Just one look in his eyes and I am his."* At that point she said as they danced she saw the palm of his hand and noticed the nail prints. Immediately she knew who he was and she thought to herself, *"Oh, I don't want this dance to stop! I want it to go on forever."* However, the dance did stop and as the music died, the man leaned over and whispered in her ear.

At this point in the seminar every eye was on this lady and with tears pouring down her cheeks, she said, *"He leaned over and whispered in my ear, 'I'm wild about you.'"*

Have you ever heard the Lord tell you that he is wild about you? Have you ever heard the Lord tell you that he is crazy about you? The truth is that he loves you so very much. There is nothing about you he does not love.

God Wants the Very Best for You

No eye has seen, no ear has heard, no mind has con-
ceived what God has prepared for
those who love him.

1 Corinthians 2:9

Do you know that God has wonderful
and amazing plans for your life?

Do you know that only you can fulfil these plans? Rise up

and take your rightful place!

Waiting on God?

Do not wait with panic or anxiety – instead wait in the place
of peace and rest! He will never fail you!

DO NOT BE AFRAID OR DISCOURAGED,
FOR THE LORD GOD, MY GOD,
IS WITH YOU. HE WILL NOT FAIL YOU
OR FORSAKE YOU!

1 Chronicles 28:20

The Lord Knows You by Name!

I t's wonderful to know that the Lord knows you by name. When I first heard God call me by name, it made me feel really special. The God of the universe knows me – WOW! He knows my name! He calls me by name! There is no mistaking his call. His message is not for someone else; it's for me! He mentions my name! He speaks my name! My name is spoken by the King of Kings! His gentle voice seems to make my name sing whilst I dance for joy. Do you know that the Lord loves you and knows you by name? Have you heard him call you by name? He speaks your name! Take time to listen and hear; the Lord God loves you and calls you gently by name.

The watchman... calls his own sheep by name.

John 10:3

I am the good shepherd;
I know my sheep and my sheep know me.

John 10:14

 Things Not to Carry
Through Life...

Guilt
(Psalm 38:4)

Fear
(1 John 4:18)

Condemnation
(Romans 8:1)

An anxious heart
(Proverbs 12:25)

Unforgiveness
(Colosians 3:13)

Worry
(Matthew 6: 25–34)

A Grudge
(Genesis 27:41/Mark 11:25)

Instead...
be carried in the arms of your God
(Isaiah 40:11)

3 Things to Guard...

Your heart
(Proverbs 4:23; Philipians 4:7)

Your tongue/mouth
(Proverbs 21:23; Proverbs 13:3)

Your soul
(Proverbs 22:5)

God's promises
and special words for you:

> *The Lord himself goes before you and will be with you; he will never leave you nor forsake you. Do not be afraid; do not be discouraged*
>
> (Deuteronomy 31:8)

God says in various parts of the Bible, *"I will never leave you nor will I forsake you!"* What a beautiful promise for all of us. We must not only believe this, but remember this in every part of our everyday life. We can so often forget that our God walks with us – and listen to this: even when we do wrong things, he is there. A witness to all our actions, but his love for us continues. He loved us before we became his son or daughter, (John 3:16 tells us that God loves the whole world - not just Christians) and he loves us now. But his love for us wants us to repent and realise that the life Jesus died for, is not a life full of wrong doings and us turning our backs on God, but a life filled with the goodness of God. He says:

"Oh my precious and wonderful child, I want you to know that my love will never falter or fade, but as you turn to me, you will experience the depth, breadth, length

and height of my love for you"

(Ephesians 3:16-19).

This is my perfect will for you. Come my love, my precious one, come and experience everything that awaits you. Know the security of knowing that I will never leave you, nor will I ever forsake you. You will never be alone! You are precious and beautiful to me. I love you now and I will always love you. Trust in me as I lead and guide you into all I have for you, my child."

You are never alone – he walks beside you – forever with you.

Hungry for Love?

One night, during the early hours of the morning, our young son, Aidan shouted, 'Dad!' As we lay in our bed, I thought to myself, 'I'm so glad he shouted Dad and not Mum!' However, Ray did not move. A few seconds later, Aidan shouted a little louder this time, 'Dad!' Ray still did not move! As I lay there I thought to myself, 'oh great, am I going to have to get up to find out what is wrong with Aidan?' Before I could move, Aidan shouted again, but this time very loudly, 'DAD!' I went to move, but before I could move a muscle, Ray was up and out of our bed. When he went into Aidan's room, our son was sitting on his bed with his arms open wide saying, 'Dad I had a bad dream and I need a hug.' Ray gave him a hug and prayed with him.

Are you hungry for love? Are you hungry for God's love? You see it was Aidan's desperation that got Ray out of his warm bed. If we are desperate for God and his love then we will be willing to put our hunger on display. It won't matter how long or how loud you have to shout as long as we know and have his presence. Ask yourself this question, 'how desperate am I for God's love?' Are you quietly shouting, 'Dad'? Or are you raising your voice a little and shouting, 'Dad?' Or are we desperate enough to be shouting from the depths of our being, 'DAD!' When we are really hungry for him, we will be willing to do anything in order to have him. When our hearts are set on desperate, our Heavenly Father will come running to show us how much he utterly loves us. He will change us with one look; he will change us with one hug!

YOU'VE STOLEN MY HEART
WITH ONE GLANCE OF YOUR EYES
AWAKENED MY LOVE
YOU'VE AROUSED MY DESIRES
YOU'VE LIFTED UP GRACE
LET ME FEEL YOUR EMBRACE
ARISE LET ME LOOK ON YOUR BEAUTIFUL,
BEAUTIFUL FACE.

Song – One from Two
Written by Ray Goudie/Mark Underdown
Published by Curious? Music UK/ngm © 2005

The following is a text I received from a close friend to tell me of a time where she had the most incredible encounter with the deep love of God. As I read it, my spirit leapt within me and my heart yearned for another encounter with our amazing God. May this stir your heart to go deeper with the King of love.

"Oh how I am loved – deeply, completely, meltingly loved! How relentless are his affections! How beautifully terrible his passion for me! How eternity-changing, heart-healing, freedom-making his jealous desire! I am completely and joyfully helpless in the face of his hurricane heart and I lie a rejoicing mess – fully undone as the King of love 'bundles' me with his violent gentleness."

The Sweet Place of Peace

There's a deep place of intimacy where each of us can go where we can experience love beyond all measure. There is a place where you will feel engulfed with the presence of God; where you feel hidden from the world. Even though there are many around you; even though you are in a crowded place, there's a quiet place of love, joy and peace that you can experience at all times. Oh the joy of being in that place, of closing your eyes and experiencing his deep and all encompassing love. To be at one with the Lord is so wonderful. I so adore that place. All requests go! All stresses and sorrows flee. In that place there is only one thing you can do and that is to speak out your love for God. As he bathes you in the sunshine of his smile, all you can do is to shout aloud in your heart how wonderful, how lovely, how amazingly beautiful he is. This is not a place to 'do', it's a place to 'be', a place to be at peace and at one with Him. As he fills you again and again with his strong yet gentle love, all you want to say is how much you love him and how he fills your life with joy. Oh how I love Jesus, my Jesus, my precious Jesus; he is so wonderful. As you speak out your love for your glorious King, the waterfall of his amazing grace soaks you through. He surrounds you with himself and it is so wonderful. Words cannot describe how amazing he is. Oh the sweet place of peace that I never want to leave. I have been to this intimate place many times; sometimes in the middle of a crowded place; sometimes in the quietness of the night. No matter where you experience God, his presence fills your heart with joy and your spirit cries out with ecstasy.

When one of our sons was young, we left him and his brother in the care of two friends while we had a couple of days away by ourselves to celebrate our anniversary. This couple did not have any children themselves at the time and when we called home to ask how they were getting on we heard them say that they were getting on well but that they had had an interesting time with our youngest son, Aidan.

He had gone for a sleep and sometime later they had decided to go and see if he was awake. They said that immediately they opened the door, the smell that hit them was overpowering but what they saw shocked them completely. Aidan had been creative with his dirty nappy and decided to take it off. He then had proceeded to paint the cot (which had many small delicately decorated wooden bars) with the contents of his nappy! Not satisfied with that, he decided that he would plaster it on his head, his body and even in his mouth! I'm sure it must have put our friends off having children for a long time. Even though our friends cleaned everything up, we were still discovering pooh on the cot some time later; it got everywhere. I felt really sorry for our friends. Somehow it is easier to cope with things like that if you are the parents of the child. I hate seeing people being sick, but when it inevitably happened to my children as they grew up, I didn't mind cleaning it up because I loved them so very much.

It's so good to know that whatever mess we get ourselves in, God loves us and willingly cleans us up so that we can start all over again.

"Come now, let us reason together," says the Lord.
"Though your sins are like scarlet, they shall be as white
as snow; though they are red as crimson, they shall be like
wool."

Isaiah 1:18

God is love.
Whoever lives in love lives in God,
and God in him.

1 John 4:16

I will sing of the Lord's great love
for ever.

Psalm 89:1

For great is your love,
higher than the heavens,
your faithfulness reaches to the skies.

Psalm 108:4

"Though the mountains be shaken and the hills be removed,
yet my unfailing love for you will not be shaken nor my covenant of peace be removed," says the Lord.

Isaiah 54:10

Know this – because of the Lord's great love we are not consumed for his compassions never fail. They are new every morning; great is his faithfulness.

Lamentations 3:22-23

Let the love of the Lord cover and surround you forever. Remember you are forever the apple of his eye.

What a Gift!

When my husband reached the BIG FIVE O I was extremely concerned that I would not be able to think of a present that seemed 'special' enough for him. So I thought I would consult the greatest creative mind in the universe – my Heavenly Dad! Whilst praying and asking God what to do, this God-inspired idea filled my mind. I would give Ray a present every month throughout the year to make his whole year special. I bought twelve cards and on each card I wrote what his present was for that month. Some months the presents were 'BIG', like a romantic trip to Paris and other months the presents were smaller like 'breakfast in bed'. Some presents were trips I had arranged to see special friends that we hadn't seen for many years because of the pressure of our work. All the presents were thought through carefully with Ray in mind. I picked presents that I knew he would love.

As I wrapped up his 'present', I was desperately hoping that I had heard God correctly. The present didn't seem very much; only twelve little cards, but so much thought, work and prayer had gone into it. The morning of his birthday arrived and although I, and our boys, Daniel and Aidan, had bought him a couple of other presents, it didn't look as though it was a present fit for a special birthday. I handed Ray his carefully wrapped up 12 cards and said *"This is your main present; I really hope you like it."* As he looked at it very curiously, I was anxiously thinking 'Oh, maybe I should have bought something else'. However, when he opened it, I was totally unprepared for his reaction. As he opened each card and read what they said, he was visibly moved and tears started coming to his eyes. When he finished, he told me it was the most special present he had ever received.

When Ray told others about his present, quite a number of friends said to their partners, *"What a great idea! Make sure you remember that idea when its time for me to celebrate a special birthday."*

When I was preparing Ray's gift, I had such fun thinking of all the presents he would like to receive and how I could make them extra special. It took a lot of time and effort, but the result was certainly worth it. I had to make phone calls, arrange flights, secret rendezvous, meals etc., without him realising what I was doing, but the effort made the event so special to Ray.

Isn't it wonderful to know that our Father God loves us much more than I could ever love Ray and that each day he loves to bless us? He is constantly thinking about us and how he can make each day of our lives special.

NO EYE HAS SEEN,
NO EAR HAS HEARD,
NO MIND HAS CONCEIVED
WHAT GOD HAS PREPARED
FOR THOSE WHO LOVE HIM.

1 Corinthians 2:9

Can We Trust God Like This?

2 Samuel 23 records King David's last words and David mentions the promises of God. He has not forgotten what God promised him – that his kingdom (his house that the Lord built) would last forever. *"Has he (the Lord) not made me an everlasting covenant – arranged and secure in every part? Will he not bring to fruition my salvation and grant me my desire? In other words, even after David was no longer King and therefore not in control, even after his death, God will see to it that his Kingdom will belong to David and his household will remain. In other words, David is saying to the Lord, "God I trust you to deliver your promise even after my death and I am no longer here!"*

Can we trust God like that? Will we at the end of our lives remember God's promises to us – that he would be with us, that he would never leave us, that he loved us from before the foundation of the world was put in place. That he has given us everything we need for life and godliness. That he promises – in my father's house there are many mansions – I go to prepare a place for you – if I go, I will come back and take you to be with me that you also may be where I am ……. are we still believing God's promises over our lives? Are we still remembering his promise to come back for us? Are we putting our faith in the fact that Jesus has died on a cross so that we could be free? Are we remembering that he is coming for us to take us to be with him forever? God's promises will not fail. Put your faith in him and in his word for they will come to pass. Woohoo!

trust

THE DANCE

by Lesley Hamilton

As a little girl I loved to dance. I spent hours alone dancing in our front room. I desperately wanted to be a ballet dancer. There was something about the way in which they moved that made me think of angels. I could almost picture them dancing around in Heaven.

As a family we attended a church where dancing was not an activity that was encouraged as a wholesome pursuit for a Christian girl. I resigned myself to the fact that it was probably better not to ask if I could go to ballet lessons rather than cope with the disappointment.

An aunty bought me a musical jewellery box one Christmas. Inside was a tiny pink ballerina doing a pirouette. I so wanted to be that ballerina! Mum and Dad never discouraged me from dancing at home but I definitely got it into my head that my dream of being a ballet dancer was never going to come true. I gradually stopped using Jesus and dancing in the same sentence and eventually the dancer was put to sleep.

I so wanted to be that ballerina!

As a teenager my love for theatre and the arts grew and at every opportunity I would go and see a production. I would be enthralled during performances of the Royal Ballet and I was often moved to tears by the whole experience. I would leave the shows I saw filled with a deep sense of regret, wishing that I could have been on stage with them.

A number of years passed, I got married and had children

and my dream lay dormant somewhere deep within me. Until one day I saw an advert for a show called 'luv esther'. It caught my attention; here was Jesus and dancing in the same sentence! I knew I had to see this show!

It was with an overwhelming feeling of anticipation and excitement when my friends and I went to see 'luv esther' in Edinburgh. Although my expectation was high, I wasn't really prepared for how professional the production would be. From the outset

I gradually stopped using Jesus and dancing in the same sentence.

I felt that I had been transported into a whole new realm of intimacy with God. I was so aware of God's presence and felt the sleeping dancer inside beginning to stir. The dancers were amazing; so full of something I had never seen in any other performance. They had energy, grace, passion and excellence, but they had more, they had something else! Suddenly it dawned on me; they were dancing for Jesus! That was my dream; to dance for Jesus. As 'Esther' began to sing the song 'For this very moment', tears began to well up and flow as the Holy Spirit touched my heart. I sensed God was about to do something deep in me.

The next day, I set about trying to find out as much as I could about ngm and Ray Goudie (the producer and writer of 'luv esther'). I went onto the website and read with interest about Ray's wife, Nancy Goudie and about her Spiritual Health weekends. I was inspired by the vision, heart and mission of ngm.

When some time later, my friend, Ruth, and I went to 'New Wine', we bought the book that Nancy had written about 'luv esther' and challenged the women at our church to use the book as a study guide for six weeks and then go and see the show when it was visiting Glasgow. Seventy women took up the challenge and this was the beginning of something special. I decided to email Nancy and let her know how much 'luv esther' had impacted my life and ask her if she would consider coming to speak to the women of our church. Nancy and a small team came up in March '07 and I met them at the airport.

When I looked at them – I could see Jesus.

As I walked towards them I was aware of the same feeling that I had as I watched the dancers at 'luv esther'. These girls were full of something which shone out of their faces. When I looked at them – I could see Jesus. They carried his presence!

I could tell by the way that Nancy and her team prayed that they were expecting the Holy Spirit to move. During that day, God impacted my life and I have not been the same since. God spoke to me again and again through what Nancy shared and through the spiritual exercises she used. I knew what I wanted; I wanted what Nancy and her team had and what I had seen in the 'luv esther' dancers. I cried out to God to go deeper with him.

Twenty five of us decided to go to Nancy's Spiritual Health weekend in Bristol. A few nights before we were due to go I had a dream. Jesus was walking with me in a garden I had never been to before. I walked with him under an archway and in front of me was the most amazing waterfall, the noise of the rushing water was almost deafening. He told me to stand underneath it and be drenched by his Holy Spirit. As I stood under the water I could smell the most beautiful fragrance. When I asked Jesus was it was he said, 'It is the rose of Sharon' (Song of Songs2:1). Jesus is the rose of Sharon and when we get close to him, we will carry the same fragrance.

A few days later we set off for Bristol; there was an amazing sense of expectancy amongst our crowd as we gathered at Glasgow airport. We were believing God for big things this weekend. I could not believe it when Nancy said during the weekend that God wanted to come and drench us in his waterfall. In fact at one point, she had a video clip of a waterfall on the screen and the noise of

I looked up into the eyes of Jesus and was captivated.

the waterfall coming through the speakers. I found it difficult to stand as I recognised my dream.

Jesus then told me to stand underneath his waterfall as he wanted to purify me and drench me in his Spirit. I could again smell the rose of Sharon. It was as if I was transported into the throne room of God and I found myself on my knees. I was aware I was in the presence of the Father and although I could not see his face, I knew he was smiling. He reached out and placed a white gold crown on my head and called me his princess. He then lifted me up and turned me around to face Jesus. Jesus was holding a pure white dress, embroidered with gold thread and encrusted with tiny coloured gem stones. He helped me put it on. I had never seen such a beautiful dress and I could not take my eyes off it. Then I heard a voice say, *"The bride eyes not her garment, but her dear bridegroom's face."* I looked up into the eyes of Jesus and was captivated. I couldn't look away. He then told me that he had something else to give to me. He bent down and placed a tiny pair of pink ballet shoes on my feet and they fitted perfectly. *"These are yours; you will dance for me,"* he said.

When I returned from Bristol, I was full to overflowing. I couldn't wait to share everything with my husband, Duncan. Next to Jesus, he is the most important person in my life and the one with whom I share everything. I danced in worship in our living room. I felt like I was five again, dancing and singing for Jesus. Woohoo!

Cry Freedom! Be who God created you to be and dance like nobody is watching!

I will soar on wings like eagles

As I was writing this book, I am doing so in Bournemouth. This is my last day and I have said to the Lord several times, *"I am overwhelmed with tiredness Lord. Show me your strength O Lord I pray."* I looked at the beautiful calm sea out of my window and then looked again at my notes and read this from the Bible:

"He gives strength to the weary and increases the power of the weak. Even youths grow tired and weary, and young men stumble and fall; but those who hope in the Lord will renew their strength. They will soar on wings like eagles; they will run and not grow weary, they will walk and not be faint."

Isaiah 40:29–31

I had heard God speak through this promise and although I was tired, I knew that God would renew my strength. I would soar like the eagle which flies higher than any other bird in nature. I would run and not grow weary and I would walk and not faint. What a wonderful promise from a faithful, incredible God.

Song of Love

The two brothers could not be more different. The older one had everything! He was clever; confident, was blessed with good looks, had lots of friends and had everything going for him. The younger brother was not clever, or good looking, in fact he had a hunchback and very few friends. He was not confident; however, he had an amazing singing voice. He used to fill the house with songs of joy.

When the brothers were at boarding school, the older brother did not want anyone to know that the boy with the hunchback was his younger brother. One day the brother with the wonderful voice was picked upon by some boys at his school. They called him names and ripped off his shirt to expose his deformed back. The older brother, who was an admired leader of the student body knew what was happening but choose not to intervene. The younger boy felt betrayed by his brother by what he failed to do. He left the school and from that day on he never sang again.

Years passed and the subject of that day was never spoken about. One day the older brother realised what he had done. He was full of remorse and travelled hundreds of miles to come home and beg his brother's forgiveness. The two brothers talked long into the night and they hugged and cried together as forgiveness flowed. During the night the older brother awoke to the sound of beautiful singing which flooded the house. His younger brother was singing again.

When we know we are loved, our heart will be full of songs of joy.

I heard a story recently about a pastor who could not cope with the stress and strain of life. The pressures upon his life were so strong that one day he left his church, his job, his home, his family, friends and his wife! He travelled by himself to a remote place in the mountains where he stayed in a little cabin. The only heat came from a very small electric fire. One day as he huddled around his little fire feeling very low, the electric heater died. It was the last straw! He kicked the electric heater in disgust and shouted at the top of his voice, "I hate you God." He then sank to his knees sobbing. As he was crying, he heard the voice of God say gently, "I know and I understand." He then heard Jesus sobbing with him.

When he heard Jesus sobbing, he got up on his feet, dried his eyes and got into his car. He drove back home to the same situation with the same problems, but he knew he could cope because he knew Jesus loved him and he was with him.

When you know how much you are loved and that you are never alone, you can cope much better with the stresses of life.

The Lord himself goes before you and will be with you; he will never leave you nor forsake you. Do not be afraid;

79

God's promises
and <u>special words for you</u>:

> *I am close to the broken-hearted and I save those who are crushed in spirit*
>
> (Psalm 34:18)

"My incredible and wonderful son/daughter, I want you to know that I have seen your tears and your weeping in the night but do not say that I have deserted you, in fact I am close to you right now. I won't ever leave you nor will I ever forsake you. I am with you and I will save you. A righteous person may have many troubles, but I will deliver them from them all (Psalm 34:19). Do not give in to your fears or condemnations from the enemy, but instead take refuge in me (Psalm 34:22) for my promise is true I am near to you and I will save you from all that crushes you. I am your strong tower and those who cling

to me are safe (Proverbs 18:11). Cling to me and know that I am with you always. Do not be afraid for I am with you (Deut 31:6)."

As I am writing this book, I am sat next to a window which looks out to the sea. In the vast distance I see a white blob on the horizon. I wonder what it is, is it a ship? As it comes nearer it is getting more and more obvious, I realise that it is a ship. In the distance it looked tiny and not able to accommodate in itself the many people on board. It takes some time to come into being, but when it does, it is huge and well able to accommodate all the people. It's the same with God's promises. When we see it or even just hear about it, it seems so small and not able to accommodate all what God has said. But as we trust in God and it comes closer he will bring it more fully into our sight and then we can see all the promises come into being. We can see what God has promised becoming a reality and know that he is more than capable of bringing it into being. In fact, it is bigger than we imagined it would be. What seemed so improbable is now clearly able to do all he has said. On board the ship are bedrooms to accommodate hundreds of people. People don't have to go over board to have a swim, in fact there are several pools so that each person can appreciate refreshment without putting themselves in danger. What seemed impossible now seems miraculous. By trusting God to show us the way of salvation, means that we can see all the promises God has promised come into being as we wait and trust in him.

There are some promises that are conditional. I realised this when God spoke to me in 1978 and promised me that he would transform my husband. I had been married to Ray, my best friend, the one I could share anything with, my beloved, for about 4 – 5 years when Ray told me that he was giving up his Christian faith. Unknown to me he had a pornography problem which he kept a secret from everyone. This secret problem made him feel like a hypocrite. He felt that God could not love or accept him as he was and therefore although he knew God was real, he decided he could not live as a hypocrite any longer. He didn't mind me attending church, but he was not going to attend church or live as a Christian anymore. As you can imagine I was devastated. I realised that I could not give up my Christian faith, even for Ray and therefore if he went in one direction and me in another, that could ultimately lead to divorce. I decided to pray and pray, but Heaven seemed to be closed to me. It was as though my prayers hit a steel barrier and never got through to God. However, I loved Ray so much that I would not give up. I continued praying and told God that I would continue to pray until he answered, but no answer was forthcoming. I was only working three hours a day and so I spent the rest of my time praying and seeking God.

Each day I would come home and get back down on my knees and plead for Ray's life. During one of my prayer times, a verse came into my mind. *"Simon, Simon, Satan has asked to sift you like wheat, but I have prayed for you, Simon, that your faith will not fail."* (Luke 22:31-32). Jesus told this to Simon Peter before he denied him three times. He was telling Peter that despite the fact that he would deny Jesus, he was praying for him that his faith would not fail and then told him, *"When you return, strengthen your brothers"* or

as he put it in John 21, *"Feed my sheep."* I took encouragement from this verse and continued to pray for Ray. I told
the Lord that I would not stop praying until he spoke. And
spoke he did.

That afternoon, as I was praying, God answered. If he had
spoken in an audible verse I would not have heard him any
clearer. He said, *"Nancy I have heard your prayers and seen
your tears. Don't cry anymore, because if you could see what
I am going to do in Ray, you would not believe it! Instead of
praying for Ray, begin to praise me for what I am about to do."*
My tears and prayers were suddenly transformed into praise
as I danced up and down our large lounge thanking God for
his promise. God had spoken, he had promised and therefore all would be well. My prayers were transformed from
that day. Even though there was no change in Ray, I began
to praise God for what he was doing and about to do.

There was one time when I was so discouraged that I
complained to God. I could not see any change in Ray and I
had praised God for what he was doing for several months.
I thought by now I should be seeing some outward sign of
change. I remember hitting my pillow in sheer frustration
and anger, then immediately repenting for doing that. God
had told me to keep praising him – he didn't say to praise
him when I saw a change, but to do that instead of pleading
in my prayers for Ray. So, I continued to praise God despite
not seeing the change I desperately wanted to see. I knew
God had promised and I also knew from reading my Bible
so many times that God always answers his promises. A
year after I had heard God speak to me, exactly to the day,
God fulfilled his promise. It was as though I got a new husband. God moved deeply in my husband's life and what God

said was so true – if I had seen the change a year previously, I would not have believed that God could move so much in my husband's life. He then called us both into full time Christian work. For 36 years Ray and I served together in leadership in a ministry that saw God bring salvation, trans-formation and healing to thousands. Wow! God is so faithful and we made sure that we strengthened the people God put in our pathway.

I'm not sure I knew at that time that praising God for Ray was a condition of the promise, but I knew God had spoken and asked me to do just that. There was no way I was going to stop praising him for what he was doing. As I praised, God honoured his promise and changed me and my prayer life too. Prayer is not just pleading for someone but it is also hearing from God and praising him for what he is going to do. There are some promises in the Bible that are condi-tional such as: Philippians 4:4-7. As we add thanksgiving to our prayers and petitions it releases faith to us and brings peace into our lives. I should say not just the peace that the world gives, but the peace that Jesus gives (John14:29) – the peace that passes all understanding. How wonderful is that? So, if your promise from God is conditional, then make sure you fulfil the conditions, not only will it release the promise to you, but it will change you in the process.

The Unforgettable Kiss!

Many years ago my husband and I started a relationship
that has lasted almost 40 years. On one of our first dates, he
picked me up in his car and drove me to the railway station.
As he parked the car on the slight hill at the entrance to the
station, he leaned over towards me and kissed me. It was to
be a kiss never to be forgotten! It was one of our first kisses
and is made very memorable by the fact that at the same
time as he kissed me, he took his foot off the brake and the
car rolled forward slowly and hit the car in front!

The first time the Lord kisses you with his love, I am sure
you will never forget it. When I was six years of age this
was the first time I remember knowing deep down that I was
loved unconditionally; it made my heart sing and my feet
dance.

Let him kiss me with the kisses of his mouth - for your
love is more delightful than wine.

Song of Songs 1:2

My Present

I had only been dating Ray for a few months when my birthday arrived! He asked me what I would like for my present. Me being a shy (!) sixteen year old replied, "Oh Ray, don't get me anything." Inside my head, I was shouting, 'Please, please get me something really nice!' Ray continued to ask me many times, but my reply was always the same!

The night before my birthday arrived and a knock came to the door. I opened it to discover Ray on the other side with this huge box in his arms. My eyes nearly popped out of my head! Wow! What has he got me? The box was covered in beautiful paper, ribbons and bows! I was completely blown away. He brought the box into my bedroom and gave me specific instructions not to open it until the next day. I complained like crazy! I told him I could never wait until the morning. If I did I would not sleep; I was too excited! He gave in and told me that if I waited up until after midnight, then and only then could I open the box.

So, my mother, who was just an excited as I was, and I waited up until midnight. We sat there counting away the minutes. It seemed to take forever to get to the stroke of midnight, however eventually it arrived! I was straight in there. I took off the ribbons and bows; I opened up the paper and then opened the huge box. I put my hand in to discover… nothing except a note which said, "When I asked you what you wanted for your birthday, you said 'nothing', so here it is… nothing!" My mum fell about laughing! I was fuming… no; actually I did think it was extremely funny.

However in between chuckling to myself, I did lie in bed that night contemplating whether that was it, or whether he would bring me something else. The next day he did arrive with an amazing watch as my present which is just as well – or else it might have been the end of a beautiful friendship!!

This funny story which shows Ray's great sense of humour, reminds me of times when I or others have been disappointed and we go through the temptation to be discouraged. We might have thought to ourselves, 'Is this it? Is this all that life has to offer?' At times throughout life it can feel as though we have opened a box where we expected much but received little! If this is the case for you, then wait until the morning! Don't give up! Though the night is dark and long, wait for the morning! Keep your eyes on God, because his love never fails, he has much for you in the morning!

Weeping may remain for a night,
but rejoicing comes in the morning!

Psalm 30:5

God's promises
and special words for you:

> *What I have said that will I bring about; what I have planned that will I do*
>
> (Isaiah 46:11b)

His word is faithful and true. You can trust him always. If God, the living God has said it, then it will happen. Trust him through the questions and trust him through the pain. What he has planned will happen. There is no doubt about it. Even when it is too late, it's not too late for him. In John 11, it tells us that Jesus didn't turn up when his best friend (Lazurus) was ill. He didn't even attend the funeral. Mary and Martha couldn't understand it. Why didn't he come? They knew Lazurus was one of his closest friends and that he loved him. So why didn't he come? When he eventually arrived Martha and Mary thought he was too late. They had loads of questions as to why he didn't turn up, but then they discovered that Jesus wasn't too late and in fact he was right on time to see a miracle happen and to do the will of the Father. If God has said it will happen, then it will happen. Trust him through the pain and the darkness to see the miracle God has planned.

What an amazing miracle!

My Beloved, I want you to know that I am faithful to all my promises. What I have said, that will I bring about. Nothing is impossible for me. Trust me for each promise and know that my heart is always faithful to you. I have many plans for you, plans to prosper you and not to harm you, plans to give you a hope and a future (Jeremiah 29:11). What I have planned for you I will do. I will always bring my plans into being, so look up and believe. Look to me and trust in me. Nothing and no one can move you out of my loving care. You are precious to me and I will always adore you. Remember, what I have said, I will bring about. What I have planned, that will I do. My love will always surround you. I am faithful to you.

How can I trust God for his promises for me to come into being?

Trusting in God for his promises to come into being involves us knowing him intimately, and therefore knowing his character and his word, The Bible. When we meet someone here on earth, perhaps someone who could become a new friend, the only way to know if what he says is true is to know his character and if he tells the truth. Sometimes people deceive us, but if we know them well, then often something will betray their inner thoughts/actions. If you look for it, you will discover the sin they are covering. The Bible says in Numbers 32:23, *"Beware your sin will find you out."* This was Moses talking to the people who had chosen to stay east of the Jordan and who had told Moses that even though their inheritance came on that side of the Jordon they would still cross the river and go into the promised land to fight against the enemies of the rest of the Israelites and would not return home until the battle had been won. Moses was warning them that if they did not do as they had promised, no one else might know but the Lord would know. Their sin of wrongdoing would be discovered and there would be consequences for that sin whether in this life or in the next (Galatians 6:7).

When we trust God for the promises in the Bible, it's important that we look to see the context of that promise. Has God said this promise to one individual, a specific group or nation, or is it a promise for all believers? Has it been spoken to us individually? If he has given his promise then he will keep it (2 Corinthians 1:18), but do make sure it is a promise for you and not one spoken to a specific group/ nation. Go back to the Lord several times and ask him to confirm to you, his promise. Also take your promise to someone who you trust and ask them to pray with you to make sure it is for you. Do also make sure you understand that God's promises can take some time to come into being.

Knowing his voice is so essential when trusting in God for his promises. I have met so many people who tell me that they can't hear God speak to them. I often ask them if they read their Bible regularly. God speaks in various ways but the most common way is through the Bible. If you are not reading it, then perhaps that is the place to start. I have read my Bible since I became a Christian at the age of 6, however, I read the Bible very differently now. At the age of six I often read the Bible by reading a few verses or a story in the Bible. Since 1979, I have read the whole of the Bible every year and it changed my life. I read the Bible through a daily Bible Reading Planner (you can buy one for yourself on my website shop – it costs 50p and it's the best 50p you can ever spend!).

Reading the whole of the Bible really changed my life. I could not have written my first book, Developing Spiritual Wholeness, if I didn't have intimate knowledge of the Bible. I was so thankful that God led me to read the whole of the Bible – it helped hugely whilst writing that book. Although the title to that book has changed to Nancy Goudie's Spiritual Health Encounters and it has also been updated and extended, it has been my best-selling book and has been re-printed many times. It is designed to help people get the most out of the Bible by helping people to study, meditate, memorise and soak in the Bible so that they can hear God for themselves. It encourages your spiritual life and your overall well-being. This book is available on my website too – nancygoudie.com.

Once you know the promise is for you, then trust God to bring it into being – he will not fail you! One of the verses I love is Joshua 21:45 – Not one of all the Lord's promises to the house of Israel failed; every one was fulfilled. If that doesn't encourage you to trust God then I don't know what will do. Trust God and add your Amen to 2 Corinthians 1:20 which says, For no matter how many promises God has made, they are "Yes" in Christ. And so through him the *"Amen"* is spoken by us to the glory of God. As this verse says – all God's promises come into being through what Jesus has done on the cross for us. He said YES and it is our response to say the AMEN. Amen means – so let it be – in other words we too say Yes to this promise.

When I was very young, my Father made a promise to me and I never forgot it. He told me that when I was 17 and I had passed my driving test he would buy me a sports car. A child holds a promise close to their heart. They believe in promises. They believe that the person who said the promise will deliver. I remember reminding my dad of his promise several times as I grew up. He never answered me, just smiled. But that smile to a little girl who loved her father meant that he was saying *"Yes"*. He hadn't forgotten! It couldn't be clearer to me. Even if he had said, *"Well…. I'm not sure Nancy, we will have to wait and see! – to me that meant yes."* Or maybe he could have said *"It's only a maybe."* To a child, that means *"Yes"*. Or even if he had said, *"Well… .I need to count my pennies – even that to me meant YES."* You see, my daddy had promised and to think of him breaking that promise was unthinkable.

I had 8 lessons and passed my driving test first time. My mum and dad had just moved house to a home much further out of town so I was glad that my dad had promised me a car. I reminded my dad again, *"Dad, I've passed my driving test, where's my promise?"* I had no doubt that my dad would remember his promise, but just in case, I reminded him several times. My dad kept his promise and gave me a car. It was not brand new, in fact it was an old beaten-up Cortina, not even a sporty one, but I didn't care, I got a car! The fact that it broke down several times a month didn't bother me as my dad paid for the tax, insurance and all the repair bills. By the end of my time with that car, I'm sure he was wishing he had bought a brand-new sports car – in the long run I'm sure it would have been cheaper!!

When the Lord gives a promise, he always remembers and he delivers it. It's quite Biblical to remind the Lord of his promise - Moses, Nehemiah, David and many more all reminded the Lord of his promise to them or to the nation of Israel. It's not that he would have forgotten, but he wants us to be actively involved in the coming promise. A child never forgets a promise, so let's remember what God has promised and make sure we remind ourselves and him that he has given his promise to us. He is coming again for you and for me.

I will never forget the day when my Lord told me that I would have another child. Ray and myself had been praying for a couple of years, *"Lord, do you want us to have another child?"* But there was no reply from Heaven. We already had our first-born child, Daniel who was about two years of age. Eventually one day, God answered so clearly. He re-plied after I had again asked him, *"Lord, please tell me am I going to have another child?"* His words spoken so clearly to me, "Hosea chapter 1 verse 6. I had no idea what that verse said. I opened my Bible and read, *"And Gomer conceived again and gave birth to a daughter."* The Lord immediately said, *"I am not promising you a daughter, but you will conceive again and give birth to another child."* My prayers were answered and with renewed vigour, my husband and myself tried to have another child. But month after month and in fact year after year, the promise did not come into being. I could not understand it. It had been the clearest word I had ever received, but God did not deliver. I took my dilemma to the person who gave Ray and myself spiritual input – Ken McGreavy.

I said, *"Ken how did I get this wrong? Was it the enemy who spoke to me?"*
"No, Nancy it wasn't."
I joked: *"I heard this on 1st April, was it God's April Fool joke?"*
Again, he said, *"No Nancy that is not it."*
I said, *"Then what is it, Ken? I don't understand."*
He was silent for a few seconds and then he said, "All I can say is, perhaps it is still to happen!"

I gasped with a huge exclaim as though trying to hide a massive joke, *"But Ken I'm over 40! My doctor wants me to take precautions because I am over 40!!!"* I felt a bit like Sarah who laughed when she was told that at 90, she was going to have another child.

I told my doctor I could not take precautions. I would not

put anything in the Lord's way that would seem as though I was not believing his promise. At the age of 43, I got pregnant and God delivered my baby boy on my 44th birthday. A healthy, brilliant, joyful boy – the best birthday present I had ever received. God had not forgotten his promise. I was asked six times by various doctors and midwives if I wanted an abortion as my son might be down syndrome because of my age. I did not take the test to find out if he was as I would never have aborted him. He was God's precious gift to me. My miracle child. My doctor told me about a year later, *"Nancy, do you realise that your son is a miracle."* I said, *"Oh yes I know."* She said, "You went through the menopause immediately after your pregnancy. It's a miracle you conceived at all."

God's promises may take some time to receive, but no matter how difficult it seems for the promise to come into being, trust him, he will not forget. If he has promised, it will come to pass. Aidan was not a down syndrome baby in fact he was perfect. How good is our God and how great are his promises. At the most difficult time, I conceived and gave birth to a beautiful, healthy boy. I am overwhelmed with thankfulness to our great and faithful God

Some of the
promises of
God for you:

Philippians
4:19

And my God will meet all your needs according to his glorious riches in Christ Jesus.

"Have I not commanded you? Be strong and courageous. Do not be terrified; do not be discouraged, for the Lord your God will be with you wherever you go!"

Joshua
1:9

Deut
31:8

The Lord himself goes before you and will be with you. He will never leave you nor forsake you. Do not be afraid; do not be discouraged.

"For I know the plans I have for you," declares the Lord, "plans to prosper you and not to harm you. Plans to give you hope and a future."

Jeremiah
29:11

Isaiah
26:3

You will keep in perfect peace those whose minds are steadfast, because they trust in you.

Isaiah 41:10

So do not fear, for I am with you; do not be dismayed, for I am your God. I will strengthen you and help you; I will uphold you with my righteous right hand.

This is what he promised us – even eternal life.

1 John 2:25

John 3:16

For God so loved the world that he gave his one and only son, that whoever believes in him shall not perish but have eternal life.

If you confess with your mouth, *"Jesus is Lord"* and believe in your heart that God raised him from the dead, you will be saved.

Romans 10:9

Romans 10:11

Anyone who trusts in him will never be put to shame.

If we confess our sins, he is faithful and just and will forgive us our sins and purify us from all unrighteousness.

1 John 1:9

John 14:3

If I go and prepare a place for you, I will come back and take you to be with me that you also may be with me where I am.

I will instruct you and teach you in the way you should go. I will counsel you and watch over you.

Psalm 32:8

Matthew 11:28

Come to me, all you who are weary and burdened and I will give you rest.

Isaiah 40:31 But those who hope in the Lord will renew their strength. They will soar on wings like eagles; they will run and not be weary, they will walk and not faint.

Isaiah 40:31

Philippians 4:13

I can do everything through him who gives me strength.

Do not be anxious about anything, but in everything by prayer and petition with thanksgiving, present your requests to God. And the peace of God, which transcends all understanding will guard your hearts and your minds in Christ Jesus.

Philippians 4:6-7

Isaiah 43:2-3a

When you pass through the waters, I will be with you. When you pass through the rivers, they will not sweep over you. When you walk through the fire, you will not be burned; the flames will not set you ablaze. For I am the Lord your God the Holy One of Israel, your Saviour.

"Though the mountains be shaken and the hills be removed, yet my unfailing love for you will not be shaken nor my covenant of peace be removed," says the Lord, who has compassion on you.

Isaiah
54:10

No weapon forged against you will prevail.

Isaiah
54:17a

If my people who are called by my name, will humble themselves and pray and seek my face and turn from their wicked ways, then I will hear from heaven, and I will forgive their sin and will heal their land.

2 Chronicles
7:14

If the Son sets you free, you will be free indeed.

John
8:36

Take delight in the Lord and he will give you the desires of your heart.

Psalm
37:4

The Kiss of God

I had just seen the amazing film, 'The Passion of the Christ'. Many parts of the film had made a deep impression on me, but particularly the place where Jesus kisses his mum. It was the only light hearted bit in the film where Jesus was making a table and there was a bit of jovial talk between them both. Suddenly, he leans over and kisses his mother on the cheek. My reaction was 'Wow, I wish Jesus would kiss me like that'.

The next morning as I thought through what I had seen the night before, in prayer I turned to the Lord and said, "I would really love it Lord if you would kiss me like that." Immediately the answer came back, "Nancy, I kiss you like that every morning!" I was stunned! Then the tears began to flow as I realised afresh how much my God loves me! My Jesus had kissed me every morning of my life and yet I had not realised it.

I want you to know this truth and even if you do know, I want to remind you. The truth remains even if you have not realised it; every morning in life the Lord gently kisses you...

... his *beloved*

About the Author

Nancy Goudie is a well-known speaker and author. She and her late husband formed the band Heartbeat in the 80's and went on to found NGM and The Inspire Arts Trust based at Caedmon (their multi-million-pound arts and music complex). Nancy has written 22 books and recorded 6 meditation CD's and 2 Bible/Prayer CD's. She has also founded Nancy Goudie's Spiritual Health Weekends for women in the UK in luxury hotels. These weekends are like no other where everyone who attends feels special from the moment they arrive. She also holds Spiritual Health Days and Retreats in various parts of the UK and beyond. She is regularly on TV/Radio and has developed her own podcast plus a new online programme for men and women. Nancy speaks at conferences, events and churches in various parts of the world.

For more information on Nancy's ministry or to book her to come to your area, please visit:

www.nancygoudie.com
or www.ngm.org.uk

Nancy Goudie's
Spiritual Health Weekends | UK

One life changing weekend in a stunning 4-star hotel!

This is a weekend like no other. It's a place for women of all ages to be pampered physically yet toned up spiritually at the same time. You will feel special from the moment you arrive to the moment you leave! Come and see for yourself what this wonderful, spectacular and unique weekend is all about. This is a God appointment for you!

Nancy Goudie has been running these luxury, unique and sensational weekend conferences for many years in 4-star luxury hotels in the UK. Why not join Nancy for: Nancy's inspiring and life-changing teaching, powerful and intimate worship from the ngm worship band, inspiring input from special guests, pampering experiences, 5 star entertainment, special individual words from God, creative optional sessions, a God perfumed prayer room and so much more!

Worried you can't afford the cost? Talk to us about spreading your payments. You can also apply for a subsidised place through our bursary scheme.

Don't miss out! This is a precious God appointment for you!

What people say:

"There is nothing else like this, it's wonderful." **J.H**

"I felt God tell me that it was a privilege to attend these weekends. When I came to the first one many years ago, the love and care I felt then is still as strong 15 years later!" **SS**

"The Spiritual Health Weekends are better than a holiday in Disneyland - I just knew I had to be there this year" **SR**

For more information and booking details
visit www.nancygoudie.com or call 01454 414880

Nancy Goudie's
Spiritual Health Retreats | UK

4 days/3 nights in stunning British countryside. One in Devon and one in the Lake District.
All Accommodation has Hot Tubs.

I want to invite you to a very special, beautiful retreat in the stunning British countryside. These beautiful cottages both in Devon and in the Lake District are complete with their own hot tubs, plus amazing leisure facilities and a spa are available in a complex on the resort (Devon resort). Set in stunning countryside, this is the perfect place to relax and be revived. These amazing retreats are only for a small amount of people.

"I am so excited about these Spiritual Health Retreats! Every conference I run, God transforms lives and does miracles, and these retreats are no different. They are a place to rest, relax and enjoy the beautiful surroundings and facilities, but they will also be a place where we can explore with a small group of people, the incredible love of God for each one of us. At both retreats we have sessions with intimate worship and inspiring teaching. Plus we have our Health and Wellbeing sessions as part of these retreats too.

We will have some optional walks and optional fitness sessions and enjoy eating together at least once.

There will be optional extras you can have including extra meals, spa treatments and optional activities as well, details of which will be available nearer the time. I would love you to join me"

Nancy x

"Got so much from this time away... thank you for a wonderful experience. God was so present!!! Loved each session... Nancy is inspirational... The attention to detail phenomenal. So, so wonderful. Thanks for everything" Delegate

"Just feel so blessed this weekend in so many ways. Just thank you doesn't seem to be anywhere near enough for how I feel – so blessed by you and thank you for such an opportunity to step out of the madness into such a relaxing space." Delegate

For more information and booking details contact Zoe Wickham at:

NGM, Caedmon Complex, Bristol Road, Thornbury, Bristol BS35 3JA
Tel: 01454 414880 **Email:** zoewickham@ngm.org.uk
Or visit: www.nancygoudie.com

Other Paperback Books and Products
by Nancy Goudie. Available at www.nancygoudie.com

The Gift of Laughter - Book 2

Do you love to laugh? Well, who doesn't love to laugh. Do you know that laughter is a gift given to us all to help us enjoy life to the full? We live in a world often full of stress, anxiety and worry and one of the ways we can navigate our way through life is by using the gift of laughter. Laughter does so many wonderful things to our bodies. Laughter is good for you physically, mentally, emotionally and spiritually. Do you know it can reduce wrinkles, help us lose weight as well as reducing high blood pressure? Experts tell us that 15 minutes of laughter can give the same benefit as 2 hours of sleep! What a gift! It's a great medicine that has incredible healing powers and the great news is that it's free and has no horrible side effects. If you are looking for tips, interesting quotes on laughter and many stories to make you laugh then this is the book for you. These stories come from every-day situations and some will make you laugh out loud.

You Are Loved

The Beatles told us in the 1960's 'all we need is love' yet so many of us still don't know what real love feels like. Many of us have experienced a love which has scarred us because it was less than true love should be. We often yearn for someone to truly love us. This book shows that you are beautifully loved and cherished. We are all born with a longing to be loved yet sometimes we feel that no one truly loves us. Yet this is so far from the truth.

If you wake up feeling miserable, unloved and life feels hard then open this book at any page and you will receive encouragement for your soul. You will read about a love that is there for you no matter what is happening in your world. The truth is that you are valued, deeply loved, cherished and protected. This book shows you how wonderful you are!

Who Would Ever Have Thought

This is the incredible story of two ordinary people from Ayr in Scotland. They lived in an idyllic and beautiful bungalow, had terrific jobs as well as a brand new sporty car, had a myriad of wonderful friendships and brilliant families too, but they left it all behind to follow God on what turned out to be an amazing faith filled journey. It's the story of Heartbeat, ngm, Caedmon – their £3 million pound arts facility, Nancy's Spiritual Health Weekends, Ray's musicals luv esther, The Prodigals and much, much more. Nancy takes you through the highs as well as the lows, yet once you've finished reading, you'll be left feeling encouraged and built up. There are many places where you will laugh and a few where you may shed a tear! This is not just a story; this is a journey that will change your life. **Also available on Amazon Kindle and audiobook (via Audible)**

Spiritual Health Encounters. (Transform and nourish your spiritual and emotional well-being).

This unique and creative book has helped thousands of people transform and deepen their walk with Jesus. This wonderful expanded book will deepen your intimacy with God and lead you to discover spiritual and physical wellbeing. Each spiritual health plan will take you on an exciting and creative journey through meditation, hearing from Heaven, writing a psalm and discovering many encounters with God. This is a tool you will not want to be without. It's great for individuals, small groups and for counsellors, church leaders/pastors to give to those who need a breakthrough. This dynamic book has changed and will continue to change lives! It's not just a book you read, it's a book you do and through it you will transform your heart, your soul, your mind and nourish your wellbeing. **Also available on Amazon Kindle.**

You Are Beautiful (hardback book)

The title of this book says it all – You Are Beautiful – Born to be Significant. Whether you are a man or a woman we are all unique, creative, wonderful, significant, valuable, and yes beautiful human beings. We all need to know how incredible we are. Each one of us was born with beauty and creativity in our DNA because each of us whether male or female was born in the image of God (Genesis 1:27). We have all been put on this planet for a purpose and a reason and therefore the truth is all of us have been born to be significant.

This book is designed to encourage and bless you. If one day you wake up feeling miserable, or at any point in the day you get a knock back from a comment someone has said about you, then pick up this book. Open it at any page and you will receive encouragement for your soul. You will hear the truth about who you are and no matter what anyone else thinks or says, you are born to be significant, and you are a wonderful, creative, beautiful human being.

Treasures of Darkness

This is a very naked and honest autobiographical account of a time when the world around Nancy started to collapse. Her husband, Ray, fell into a dark pit where he experienced ill health and burnout. At the same time God was taking their ministry, ngm, through a shift, which caused much pain and insecurity and led to many people eventually leaving. Pressures swept in like a storm leaving devastation, confusion and unanswered prayers. Nancy discovered that through this time there were *'treasures of darkness and riches hidden in a secret place'* (Isaiah 45:3).

Confident? (hardback book)

This book is for anyone who sometimes swings from being confident to feeling a failure. It's a book full of encouragement, wise words, poems, songs and stories to lift your spirit and get you back on your feet again, ready to face life once more. Through its pages you will feel accepted, really loved and realise afresh how amazing you are!

You are Special (hardback book)

In our culture of stress with so much pressure to look good and be famous, we often need to be reminded just how unique, precious, remarkable and extraordinary we are! No matter what colour our skin is, what size we are, what intelligence we display, what background we come from, the truth is each of us is an exceptional human being. In every page of this book you will discover the truth about yourself and realise afresh that you are deeply loved, special and accepted.

Oasis of Hope (hardback book)

There are times in our lives when we all need an oasis, a place where we can go and receive a thirst quenching drink for our souls. This book is such a place! A place where hope is renewed and faith can begin to grow. A place that will help refresh the reader physically, mentally, emotionally and spiritually. A place that gives us more of what we need to enable us to keep on going in our journey through life. It is designed to plant seeds of hope into the barren places of our hearts and encourage those seeds to grow and develop so that our faith will soar.

Oasis of Delight (hardback book)

There are times in our lives when we need an oasis, a place where we can go to receive a thirst quenching drink for our souls. This book is an exploration of what it means to live in the oasis of delight, tasting its fruit, relaxing and relishing in the lush surroundings; free to explore and enjoy the depths of his fulness of joy and his pleasures forevermore. It inspires us to enjoy the delightful fruit of intimacy with God, whilst all the time pointing us towards the day when we will be in the ultimate garden of delight for eternity.

The Best Is Yet To Come Journal (hardback)

This fantastic journal has a page of inspiration from Nancy and plenty of pages for your notes, prayers, drawings etc. Printed with a luxury finish this is the ideal journal for you – grab your copy now.

Our Greatest Adventure

This book tells a story of courage in the midst of pain, peace in the midst of sorrow and trust in the midst of confusion. It's a story of love and devotion in the midst of one of the biggest challenges Ray and Nancy Goudie have ever known. It's the story of God's faithfulness when Ray was diagnosed as having pancreatic cancer and of God's continued faithfulness and immense presence when Ray walked through the valley of the shadow of death and eventually fell asleep into the arms of Jesus. This is an honest, deep and raw story that will touch your emotions, making you laugh as well as cry. There are many funny and humorous moments amidst the pain and the heartache. It's a story that will fuel your faith in God and ignite your passion for his presence. This is a story that many have said had to be told. **Also available on Amazon Kindle.**

All books are available direct from ngm at:

www.ngm.org.uk, www.nancygoudie.com

Meditation CDs

Smile

If you are feeling the daily stresses of life, the busyness of work, the pressures of family or just need some soothing for your soul, then this is recording for you. **Also available to download from iTunes and other online platforms.**

Meditations for the Beloved

We all need to know we are loved and valued. This incredible music and mediation CD will take you to the secret place where you will know you are The Beloved; you will be overwhelmed with love, feel accepted and experience a peace that passes all understanding. **Also available to download from iTunes and other online platforms.**

Speak...Declare the Truth: Vol 1

Are you feeling overwhelmed? Are circumstances or people getting you down? Are you in need of encouragement? Do you need to know you are loved? Do you need to see a miracle of health or provision? Does everything seem impossible for you? Then I have news for you! The Bible says in 2 Peter 1:3 that God has already given you everything you need for life and godliness. Not just some things, but everything you need. We need to start reading, believing and confessing the truth. This CD helps you to do just that!

What we speak has power and therefore when we confess the truth contained in the word of God, power is released and the word brings life. Speak life and truth into your circumstances and let's see God do a miracle! **Also available to download from iTunes and other online platforms.**

Speak...Declare the Truth: Vol 2

Do you know you are loved? Do you realise you are valued? Do you understand you are special? So many of us struggle with confidence, our self-image and our mental ability to believe we are worthy. We don't value ourselves and therefore we cannot see how anyone else will value us. Do you know God delights in you and celebrates you? Do you realise that he sings songs of joy and delight over you? Do you struggle with the ability to see a joyful future full of hope? God not only believes in you but he has wonderful plans and purposes for your life. Who are you listening to? Who are you believing? We need to listen to the truth of the word of God rather than listening to the lies of the enemy.

There is power in the spoken word, so read, believe and confess the truth and see your circumstances and your life change for the better. **Also available to download from iTunes and other online platforms.**

All meditation cds are available direct from ngm at: www.ngm.org.uk, www.nancygoudie.com

Other Products

Bible Reading Planners

A superb way of systematically reading through the Bible in one or two years.

Wholehearted - Leanne Goudie

Wholehearted is a 30-day interactive devotional written by Leanne Goudie and packed full of encouragements, scriptures and space to journal. So many women go through life struggling to embrace their God given identity and worth, so Wholehearted was written to encourage and equip women in their everyday lives.

Throughout the book there is space to journal and write, allowing you to process anything that arises from reading the encouragement given each day. This is your devotional and your space to process, so take it at your own pace and enjoy the journey of living your life. Grab your copy now! **Only available on Amazon Kindle.**

Rooted - Leanne Goudie

Rooted was created to help you delve deeper into what it is to truly trust God and encourage you to look at how you can live a life of complete faith in Him. Throughout there is space for you to journal and process anything that arises from reading the encouragement given each day. This is your devotional and your space, so take it at your own pace and embrace the journey of becoming more and more 'Rooted' in your faith!

Breathe - Leanne Goudie

Breathe is the third 30-day interactive devotional written by Leanne Goudie. It is packed full of encouragements, scriptures and journal space. In a world that feels like it never stops, there is an increasing need to find rest in his presence, to know whose we are and to capture the anxious thoughts that can so easily take control if we let them.

This devotional is a guide to help you to discover more of His peace and rest on a daily basis whilst also encouraging you along the way. Let's take on this journey together and discover more of His peace, love and stillness together!

Living Life As You Were Created To Be - Zoe Wickham

In a world where social media and TV has such influence, and when we can be switched-on 24/7, we need to not only know who we are created to be, but learn to live life in the image of our creator, even when challenges and distractions face us.

Jesus said in John 10:10b *"I have come that they may have life and have it to the full."* What does that mean? We can easily interpret this verse as saying we need to do lots of things. I believe this verse means that we can have a life with Jesus, fully living out who he has created us to be and what he has called us to do. When we get to that place, life is really exciting, and we can overcome our problems with Jesus!

I know so often life can pull us down, our identities can be bashed, and we can lose our way. Knowing and keeping our identity with Jesus is such an important key to living our lives to the full. Join me on this 28-day journey as you discover who you are, whose you are and how you can live your life to the full with God.

One Woman's Guide to Life - Zoe Wickham

At the time of writing this book I am 43 years old. I haven't lived all my years but I feel I have lived enough, and learned some life lessons the hard way, so I want to share them with others. My heart is that you will find freedom in these pages, you will be free to express who you were born to be, you will discover it's not too late to change things no matter what age you are, you will learn to take care of yourself and learn also that it's okay not have all the answers. I have read a lot of self-help books (there's nothing wrong with them) in the journey of trying to improve myself, but this isn't one of those. This is an honest account from a wife, a mum, a woman who has lived her first 40 plus years and wants to share with you some of the highs and lows to help you to find balance, happiness and joy in life and that you might learn to live life more fully!

NGM Worship - Unbreakable Love

Unbreakable Love featuring the beautiful vocals of Leanne and Esther. This is a great ep with some fantastic new songs, plus a re-release of the track Heal Our Nation from Heartbeat. Do make sure you grab your copy for yourself and for your family/friends! **Also available to download from iTunes and other online platforms.**

All of these products are available direct from NGM at: www.ngm.org.uk, www.nancygoudie.com

NANCY GOUDIE CONTACT DETAILS:

Should you wish to contact Nancy,
then you can write to her at:

nancy@nancygoudie.com

The NGM Trust,
Caedmon Complex,
Bristol Road,
Thornbury, BS35 3JA

Facebook: Nancy Goudie
Twitter: @nancygoudie
Instagram: @nancygoudie
YouTube: Nancy Goudie – NGM Trust

If you wish to find out more about anything in the book
or request prayer you can call: 01454 414880

For more information on Nancy and all she is doing
visit www.nancygoudie.com